Eat, Play, Poop

LETTERS TO MY PARENTS FROM CAMP

ALEC PECHE

JBSW Publishing

Acknowledgments

I'd like to thank Ellen Falk for editing this book. She usually edits my mystery novels, but she did an awesome job with Joey's letters contained therein.

Introduction

Eat, Play, Poop is the creation of mystery author Alec Peche. My community service is providing a home for neighbor dogs while their owners are away. I have a large and friendly rescue dog that accommodates dog visitors of all sizes.

I frequently dog sit my friend's dog, Joey who was adopted through Best Friends Animal Sanctuary in Kanab, Utah. While I always send dog parents pictures of their dog having a good time at my house, Joey's parents also get a text. Those texts grew into letters from camp enjoyed by their friends and family.

Now I'm introducing Joey to the world through a series of pictures and letters. I hope you enjoy these stories written in the voice of a pre-teen boy.

By the way, the pictures and text are not centered and I'd like to blame Joey for that even though I spent days trying to get it perfect. I hope you'll laugh at some of these stories as a this dog's world is always happy.

～

Dear Mom and Dad,

I'm at Camp Daniel and I've spent six hours chasing squirrels and I have nothing to show for it, but I'm still a happy dog.

Love, Joey

～

～

Dear Mom and Dad,

I saw pictures of where you're hiking and I'm happy to stay home on my soft bed. I know you can't read my letters as the postman doesn't deliver where you're hiking. At Camp Daniel, I have a bunkbed. I have the upper bunk and my friend Daniel has the lower bunk. I don't understand why you don't want to take me on your hike.

Love, Joey

～

~

Dear Mom and Dad,

We picked up a new dog yesterday. We have to walk slower so it can keep up. We keep having our chains yanked to make sure we don't pee on the little thing. I know you have raised me to love all dogs regardless of their color or breed, but small dogs are a pain. They do everything slowly. They walk slow, they chew slowly—you should see how long it takes them to eat a skinny rawhide. It's ridiculous. What is really awful is they don't chase squirrels. How can you be a dog and not chase squirrels? Anyway, the small camper is only here for two days, so tomorrow it'll be just me and my buddy Daniel chasing squirrels again.

Love, Joey

~

~

Dear Mom and Dad,

Camp continues to be a blast. This is my favorite position. I can hear the squirrels in the redwood trees, protect the camp's peach tree from those nasty vermin, and yet hear the sound of the treat bag being opened inside. The meals here are plentiful and delicious. Hope you're having a good time hiking that boring mountain. See you soon.

Love, Joey

~

~

Dear Mom and Dad,

I'm writing this letter knowing that you're picking me up from camp later today. I thought I'd tell you why I am so happy here. The owner unlocks the camp door around 5:30 in the morning. As long as I keep quiet, I can start hunting for the squirrels early. She also fuels me up with two cookies, so I have the energy to chase those vermin. Presently I'm on patrol for what's happening outside of the camp. She has a special chair for me so I can be comfortable while I'm on patrol. Now is a special time of anticipation. She's going to feed me within the next half hour—lots and lots of food. See you later today.

Love, Joey

~

~

Dear Mom and Dad,

I've been sitting in this chair and looking lost at the window ever since you left last night and waved goodbye. Just kidding! I've already chased ten squirrels this morning, had a big breakfast, and been for a walk. Life is good at camp.

Love, Joey

~

～

Dear Mom and Dad,

The first picture is of me and my fellow camper in a food coma, as that's what happens when I have a full belly. The second picture is me and my fav camper practicing neck exercises. Our counselor says it's so we can hunt squirrels longer. She also says it helps with a double chin. What's that?

Love, Joey

～

~

Dear Mom and Dad,

Today I'm going to tell you about pee-mail. When me and fellow camper Daniel cruise the neighborhood, we catch up on the gossip via pee-mail. Linda (that's our counselor's name) doesn't give us much time to read before she yanks our leashes to move on. I really have to be fast reading the message because if Daniel reads it before I do and has a comment, then I better get out of the way. If we like the pee-mail, we lick it. If we don't like it, we pee on it.

Love, Joey

Pee-mail speed reading is good for the dog mind! [Dad]

He has to read fast because if Daniel dislikes the pee-mail, then he lifts his leg and doesn't care if he pees on Joey while he's still reading. [Linda]

~

~

Dear Mom and Dad,

There's this one nearby neighborhood where all the ladies call me names. This morning this one lady walking her dog, who might I say was out of control and was giving me dirty looks, called me grumpy! Can you believe that? All I was doing was giving the stink eye to her dog. Oh well, I'll leave nasty comments about that other dog through pee-mail.

Love Mr. Grumpy

Oh boy. Sometimes people can be as grumpy as dogs. [Mom]

Mr. Grumpy needs to promote himself on social media. [Dad]

~

~

Dear Mom and Dad,

This is my happy spot! Well, except for when you're giving me a belly rub or a full bowl of food. Me and Rocky made eye contact and I told him who's boss. Later he sent his friend, Rockstar, and we made the same eye contact. Can you believe they stole peaches off the camp tree and threw the pits at me? Even after we established eye contact. That's why I hunt these evil vermin.

Love, Joey

Those rude, taunting squirrels; hopefully they get the runs from the peaches! [Dad]

~

Dear Mom and Dad,

I learned a new trick today for my fellow camper, Daniel. Linda gave us both bones and I resisted chewing mine so I could tease Daniel and make him watch me enjoy it. That was a lot of fun.

Love, Joey

Wow, sounds like you have finally figured out what Daniel has been doing, Joey! Great pics! [Mom]

Joey is cute and a schemer! [Dad]

I was surprised he had the self-control to wait.🤣 [Linda]

We have been working on his impulse control. Clever guy; he's using it in creative ways! [Dad]

~

~

Dear Mom and Dad,

I was on a lazy walk but it was the peace before the storm, or maybe I should say I before I turned into Cujo. I couldn't help myself—that fake black husky with the blue eyes had the nerve to make eye contact with me. Never look into Cujo's eyes. My raised fur and snarls were enough to make the owner hustle away with Badger, that damn husky. Aren't you proud of me?🤣

Love Cujo

That damn husky sounds like a problem😄 [Dad]

Thanks Dad, I'm happy you have my back. [Joey]

Glad to see Joey made it home again after the kerfuffle. Some dogs can really be a nuisance.😄 I think the deal with Joey is not to make eye contact with him. He was aggressive toward Frosty, a white miniature schnauzer, and I found that curious as she was the same size as Snowball, but Frosty was staring at Joey and nothing gets his hackles up like that. [Mom]

Need to work on Joey being okay with the stink eye. [Dad]

~

Dear Mom and Dad,

This is a picture of me sitting in the most perfect place on earth. They open the doors early at camp, so it's 6:15 AM and I'm in place to chase those squirrels. What's even better is that Linda has the kitchen window open so I can hear my favorite sound—the tinkle of food hitting my purple dish. That's the dinner bell for me!

Love, Joey

~

Dear Mom and Dad,

I'm late writing my letter today. Some days I have so much fun that Linda forces me to sit down and write these letters. The first picture is my face saying "I want to go for a walk." That's just for your knowledge. There's nothing better than stretching out on the cool grass early in the morning after I've had breakfast. On our first walk today, I didn't encounter any hostiles so I could smile the whole way home.

Love, Joey

Funny, but I should probably tell Joey that he IS the hostile! [Mom]

Nonstop action! Joey's gotta love it! He sure loves life! [Dad]

∽

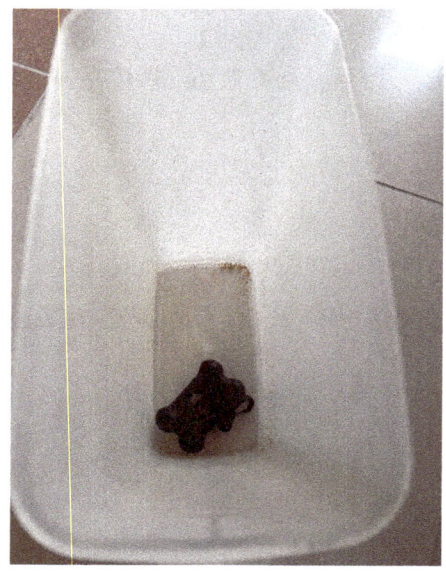

≈

Dear Mom and Dad,

The first picture is of my empty lunchbox and my poop bag container. Linda says there's a connection between the two items. My pal Daniel says he'll share his lunchbox with me so I won't starve until you pick me up from camp. His mom puts different stuff in his lunchbox, so I'm excited to try something different. The second picture is Daniel's face after we played for a while out on the grass. I included a video of our play so you can see that I'm having fun.

Love, Joey

≈

~

Dear Mom and Dad,

Me and my fellow camper Daniel like to roll around on the grass and beat each other up. Mostly we just get spit on each other. When I'm not playing I'm listening to the morning sounds of birds and squirrels. It's a great way to wake up at camp. Yesterday Linda spoke to a neighbor, and she was excited about my upcoming book called Eat, Play, Poop. Do you think the left side of my face, or the right side, is better for a book cover?

Love, Joey

Sounds like camp can't get any better! I think the name of the book is perfect! Either side of your face is good, Joey, but share that book cover with your camp mate! [Mom]

~

～

Dear Mom and Dad,

Every day at camp we have time for a nap. I love my naps and you can see how happy I am when I wake up from one. Linda took a picture of this redwood tree that hosts those vermin squirrels really high up in the branches. That's why me and my buddy are on patrol.

Love, Joey

～

～

Dear Mom and Dad,

Today we went on a new walk. Here, me and Daniel were checking out pee-mail. It's hard to do when you don't know who Skyler, Buddy, or Rusty is. If I'm going to read pee-mail, then I want to stay up-to-date on the same group of dogs. All I learned was that Skyler barks a lot and my fellow dogs were prevented from getting a good night's sleep because of his big mouth.

Love, Joey

Ahhh...the Canine Social Network! Hope Daniel and Joey send a pee-mail back letting those dogs know the 411! Another wonderful day at camp! [Dad]

～

~

Dear Mom and Dad,

As you can see, I'm in a food coma. I want to tell you about a great practice here at camp. When Linda cooks chicken breast, she saves the broth to put on our dog food. OMG, it's the difference between a dry cheeseburger and one with secret sauce on it. Feel free to continue that practice when I come home.

Love, Joey

~

Dear Mom and Dad,

This is going to be a long letter since it's my last day at camp for a while. I started with a picture of Lightfoot Leticia or Lenny. I'm not sure whether it's a girl squirrel or a boy squirrel since they smell the same, but they ran the length of fence three times. It was so exciting but now the squirrel is winded and so is my camp partner, Daniel. The next picture is me playing tug-of-war with Daniel. This was a gentle game rather than the violent snarling and biting that I usually like. I was going to send you a picture of the forlorn look I've been giving our counselor each evening, but I don't have the right image. It's my hint that I want to go to the dog gathering, but she won't take me. In case you're wondering, I'm happy to come home if only to go to the nightly dog gathering.

See you later,

Love, Joey

~

Dear Mom and Dad,

By now you're done with that skydiving thing. I don't think I would try skydiving even if you threw a squirrel out in front of me. I can catch them on the ground, so there's no reason to chase one out of an airplane. Camp's been good today—minutes after I arrived a squirrel jumped back and forth between two birch trees. I love when the entertainment starts as soon as I arrive.

Love, Joey

~

≈

Dear Mom and Dad,

I know I'm only gonna be at camp overnight this time, but already it's raining cookies here! I forgot my allergy hotspot thanks to the cookies. I admit I did run out of the cabin to hide when Linda pulled out some anti-itch cream—no thank you, just give me cookies to forget my itching.

Love, Joey

≈

~

Dear Mom and Dad,

This is me before sunrise. I've mentioned before how I love that the doors open early at camp. Think of how much good I could do in my own neighborhood if I was ridding it of vermin before sunrise? The squirrels are up early and so should I be.

Love, Joey

P.S. I've already started the day with a humongous breakfast. I love camp. 🧡

~

～

Dear Mom and Dad,

One of the things I like about camp is the no-purple policy. What, you ask? Linda gives me enough dog food to make sure there's no purple showing on the bottom of my dish. I love my dog food. I'm telling you this in case you wonder why I always gain a little weight at camp.

Love, Joey

～

＿～＿

Dear Mom and Dad,

Linda took my friend Daniel and me for a walk, and something called "fog" this morning was everywhere. I'm squinting into the distance, trying to see any vermin. I know I'm supposed to be 100% mutt according to my DNA profile, but whatever heritage I have, my strong suit is not my nose. Sure, I can smell treats from a great distance, but darned if I can smell a squirrel in the fog.

Love, Joey

＿～＿

Dear Mom and Dad,

Despite the happy look on my face, I am not enjoying camp right now. Linda hasn't taken me for a walk for 36 hours. She's walking funny around the house. It's taking her forever to get up and down the stairs. Can you believe she expects me to entertain myself with squirrels in the backyard? Does she not know how quickly I'm bored with that? Hopefully she'll be on the mend soon so I can get back to reading pee-mail.

Love, Joey

Dear Joey, play more with Daniel [Mom]

≈

～

Dear Mom and Dad,

This is my favorite time of the day. I'm in a food coma along with my good friend, Daniel. We both had awesome food, went outside and took care of nature, and then returned to fall asleep to dream of a bottomless dog food bowl. Life is good.

Love, Joey

～

Dear Mom and Dad,

I'm looking worried in this picture because Linda is yelling at her TV. She's watching something called football and I don't understand why she's mad at her screen. She has assured me that she's not mad at me, but it's kind of scary as I have never heard her voice raised in this manner before. She tried to console me that we would go for a walk soon, but she's still yelling at the screen.

Love, Joey

~

~

Dear Mom and Dad,

I thought you'd like this action shot of me playing with my good friend at camp, Daniel. We do this several times a day and Linda says it's good exercise for us as you can see from this action shot. I have my mouth around my friend's neck. Man, does he have a thick neck.

Love, Joey

Great pic! Certainly a win-win! Joey gets a chew toy and Daniel gets a massage! [Dad]

~

～

Dear Mom and Dad,

I've just ate and dawn is arising. Did you know that most vermin are active at dawn? Think of how many squirrels I could chase if only you would take me out at dawn. Let's try that tomorrow when I'm home with you.

Love, Joey

Dear Joey,
    That sounds like a swell idea! We'll let your mum take that on because she is the Special Projects Coordinator! Keep the neighborhood safe! Love ya. [Dad]

Dawn sounds like a beautiful time of day, but since the neighborhood is now safe, maybe we can give the 🐿️s a bit of time to themselves. They need their quiet time too and I'm happy to help them get it! [Mom]

～

~

Dear Mom and Dad,

I was so excited last night as Linda left the dog door open. It was three in the morning, and I went out to camp under the stars. Just me, the grass, and 40° which suits my fur coat, or maybe you would call it a sleeping bag. I wondered why Linda didn't yank me back inside like she usually does. Well, now I know why. On Wednesday morning at 3:30 the sprinklers go on. I had to run inside the house before that water hit me. So much for life under the stars.

Love, Joey

~

~

Dear Mom and Dad,

My memoir is titled Eat, Play, Poop, so I had to get at least one picture of my poop. When we go on walks to see Linda's mother, I have my favorite place in the entire world to poop. It's up on the hillside, so I can still see the squirrels while I take care of business. Better still, it's close to a garbage can which Linda appreciates. Happy Thanksgiving, Mom and Dad. You should save some treats for me.

Love, Joey

~

≈

Dear Mom and Dad,

I want to introduce you to the neighborhood terrorist. His name is Gizmo. My camp buddy, Daniel, chased him once, and now they despise each other. When I walk by with Daniel, and the terrorist is outside, I add growls and boxing steps to threaten the little fanatic. Still, he stands tall, not intimidated by the muscle and power of us two campers. Sigh.

Love, Joey

What a good-looking terrorist! [Mom]

What a sinister-looking being! [Dad]

≈

≈

Dear Mom and Dad,

I'm sending this picture to you as I think it's a great picture to put in your Christmas card. My hair is perfectly combed around my eyes and mouth. Even my fellow camper says I look handsome. I like how my fur fits with the color of the gravel as I can hide from squirrels while spying on them.

Love, Joey

≈

Dear Mom and Dad,

I'm pouting because we had to spend overnight at Linda's mother's house. I don't like it as much as at camp because the squirrels are not as plentiful as there. There's nothing to entertain me. I can't watch from an upstairs window and see the entire neighborhood cause there's only one story. Linda put this nice bed outside for me to lay on, but I stuck to my guns and stayed lying in the bushes. When her back was turned, I went over to the comfortable bed and went back to sleep. Still, she caught this picture of me through some blinds.

Love, Joey

~

~

Dear Mom and Dad,

We're back at Linda's house now, and when I looked out the window from my second-story perch, I saw a terrifying monster across the street. Linda was on a video call and didn't get her phone out to snap a picture. So I copied one from the Internet for you so you could see the monster I saw. He ran down the sidewalk, then crossed the street, and I think he went into the neighbor's backyard. I lost my mind over the monster and quickly ran down the stairs and outside to bark and let him know he better not come into my backyard.

Love, Joey

~

~

Dear Mom and Dad,

I'm standing in the rain at camp because I can. I'm always on squirrel patrol. Unlike me, the squirrels seem to be hiding from the rain. I'll stay on patrol because they have to come out at some time for food, and when they do, it's game on. I'll chase them for all I'm worth.

Love, Joey

~

~

Dear Mom and Dad,

Linda says "Happy New Year." It was a dark and stormy night. It was so dark and stormy that she couldn't photograph my walk last night. It was great, though. The wind was howling, the rain was falling sideways, and I found the perfect place to poop. I don't think Linda was thrilled with having to find it in the dark. My camp buddy Daniel also wasn't thrilled, as he just wanted out of the rain.

Love, Joey

~

Does anyone else think about murder and Mayham while walking their dog? It's the life of a writer! 🤣

TikTok
@authoralecpeche

～

Dear Mom and Dad,

Linda has been taking videos of me and my pal, Daniel. She's been uploading them to TikTok. Complete strangers are loving my videos! Just wait till my book comes out! I'll be famous by this time next year. It's all a dog's life.

Love, Joey

～

~

Dear Mom and Dad,

Linda was up late last night, so I didn't get my usual morning snack at 5:30. In fact, I was starving by the time I got it at 7:30. She redeemed herself by taking us on a nice walk around the neighborhood. I found the perfect place to poop. It was right on top of a bunch of twigs because there's no leaves on the bush at the moment. Linda was unhappy that my poop was so hard to pick up. All I knew was it was the perfect place to squat!

Love, Joey

~

~

Dear Mom and Dad,

This has been the best of mornings at camp. This morning Linda left me alone in the house with a cookie and took my bunk mate Daniel on a drive. Turns out he had to get his rabies shot, so I'm glad I missed that car ride! Linda felt bad about my friend having a needle stuck into his rump, so she took him to the local coffee shop where he got "pup-a-chino." Fortunately, he doesn't like to eat in the car, so when they got home, he shared it with me. Life is good when you can share a good cup of whipped cream with your bunk mate. Linda followed that up with shish kebab rawhide sticks for us. This is a picture of me grinning while I chew into this delight! Maybe you could take me to the coffee shop, so I won't have to share a pup-a-chino with another dog.

Love, Joey

~

~

Dear Mom and Dad,

I missed you last night. The wind was howling, the windows were shaking, and the trees were swaying. I don't mind rain, cold, or snow, but wind is really scary. It sounds angry to me, and I don't like angry things around me. Fortunately, this morning we had a great walk and I'm not worried about the wind any more.

Love, Joey

~

~

Dear Mom and Dad,

I was sad when you left last night, but guess what? The squirrel circus began early and me and my camp buddy Daniel got to watch the high-wire act of squirrels leaping in the air from tree to tree. We both stand underneath the branches, hoping the acrobats will miss and end up in our mouths. Alas, we go hungry every time.

Love, Joey

~

~

Dear Mom and Dad,

The camp was in the middle of a windstorm. To be frank, I don't like wind. I can walk in it, and I can poop in it, but I don't like to hear the cabin walls rattle with the wind. Yesterday Linda pulled out her boombox—I think she called it her "iPhone." She played something called the Rolling Stones, Beyoncé, Adele, and Imagine Dragons. It was perfect music to snooze to. I love Linda.

Love, Joey

~

~

Dear Mom and Dad,

Did you know they have a spa at camp? It offers massage services. I can't get it every day, but they offer the most relaxing belly rubs. I just close my eyes and think back over my day and all the squirrels that I nearly captured. I am in bliss.

Love, Joey

~

Dear Mom and Dad,

I think one of my favorite parts of camp is the windows. I can stay dry and warm on the inside and yet still be on patrol for any vermin across my property. I have a nice rug thoughtfully provided by Linda next to my door to the outside. In the bunk room upstairs, I have a chair that is the perfect height to keep watch on the neighborhood. I've attached an action shot of me, detecting vermin and exiting through the dog door to chase them down. In case you want to know, I'm good at my job.

Love, Joey

~

Dear Mom and Dad,

Pssst, I have a secret. I don't think Linda reads my letters before she mails them. I discovered a secret service at camp. If I go out in the rain, which I don't mind at all, Linda will give me a massage with a towel when I come back in. Is that not the coolest secret ever?

Love, Joey

~

~

Dear Mom and Dad,

You would not believe your eyes if you had seen me in camp this morning. Would you believe Linda had to call me in to eat breakfast? I was having such a good time out in the forest chasing squirrels. In fact, when I did come in, I only ate about half of my food before I rushed back outside to make sure the vermin hadn't taken over the forest while I was inside eating. Then I remembered my camp buddy, Daniel, and thought I better get inside and finish my breakfast before he gets it. You'll be happy to know I'm back outside in the forest on guard duty with a full belly.

Love, Joey

~

~

Dear Mom and Dad,

This is a picture of me and my camp buddy, Daniel, in our bunkbeds. For once, I included a picture of the resident cat, Lucy. Daniel is quite a snorer. I often fall asleep to the sounds of what I imagine a dragon sounds like when it's breathing. It's very soothing. The cool thing is, the dragon can be snoring one moment, and if I stand up on my bunk and look out the window because I see something, he immediately wakes up and he's ready to join me in a vermin-chasing adventure! Linda says you're in the mountains, but that's okay. I have all that I need here—food, love, friendship, and squirrels.

Love, Joey

~

~

Dear Mom and Dad,

This is a picture of me on squirrel patrol in the rain. I don't mind the rain at all, and the camp counselor says that's because of my thick coat. My camp buddy, Daniel, has a lot less fur than I do, and he gets annoyed with each big drop of rain hitting his face. Linda said you were in Colorado. You know you could take me there next year as I love the cold. Maybe you could find one of those sleds and I could pull something across the snow while I chase squirrels? Linda told me that was a bad idea as there were moose in the area. She said the moose are 10 times bigger than my camp buddy. Still, it might be fun to run for my life away from something so big.

Love, Joey

~

~

Dear Mom and Dad,

You might wonder why I'm sending you this picture. I had to laugh inside when Linda complained that I like to pick the most complicated spaces to poop in. She said if I would poop on a concrete sidewalk, it would be a lot easier to pick up. But I choose places with leaves, sticks, or rocks, which makes it hard to pick up all the poop according to her. Since I've never picked up my own poop, I don't know if she's right, but I'm not changing my practice. I have to have the right smell and the right urge to poop where I do. The end.

Love, Joey

~

~

Dear Aunt Lori and Uncle Stan,

I've been a very gracious host at camp to Joey. Today, it's really cold and the my Mom is making me stay outside. She put my sweater on so I would be warmer. Joey, wouldn't stop laughing at my lovely sweater. When we were wrestling, he even had the nerve to grab it. We can't all be covered in heavy fur like he is.

Unhappily, Daniel

~

Dear Mom and Dad,

I've enclosed a picture that my counselor took of me doing my tree dance, or that's what she calls it. I stand on my hind legs, paws on a redwood tree, and wiggle my butt and tail. I do the tree dance whenever I see a squirrel up there. Sometimes I get exhausted dancing, so I have to return to all four paws and just look up.

Love, Joey

≈

~

Dear Mom and Dad,

Linda captured this picture of me using my new strategy of squirrel chasing. If I sit unmoving among the plants, the squirrels can't see me until the last moment. Then I can pounce. What do you think? Am I hidden? I'm quite proud of myself for thinking of this idea.

Love, Joey

That's my boy, always thinking outside of the box! He does a good job of being a statue! [Dad]

Statue, yes, but maybe not aware that the top part of his body is visible.😂 [Mom]

~

Dear Mom and Dad,

Most of the time I think my camp buddy, Daniel, is a great friend and playmate. However, he is super-strange about bones. You can see in this picture a bone that's close to my foot—our counselor placed it there for the picture. However, as soon as the picture is snapped, I get the death stare from Daniel. I quickly jump out of my bunkbed, and he removes the bone from the chair. His death stare is so scary that I'm afraid to get back in my bunk unless Linda moves the bone toward her. Thankfully, she knows all about Daniel's death stares and helps me get into my bunk.

Love, Joey

~

Dear Mom and Dad,

This is my favorite time of the day as I think I told you in my previous letters. It's 5:15 AM and the camp operator is at work at her desk. I've had four cookies and a drink of water, completed my surveillance of the forest in the dark, and now I'm back inside to take a nap. Life is good.

Love, Joey

~

~

Dear Mom and Dad,

Daniel and I discovered some gourmet grass today. I think the human version is called angel hair pasta. It was thin, fragrant, and delicious. Linda waited patiently while we munched. Better still, she was pleased that it didn't give us gas later that day.

Love, Joey

~

~

Dear Mom and Dad,

I feel like I'm getting too old to keep writing these daily letters to you, so I thought I would end with one of the most common pictures of me at camp. I'm under a coastal redwood tree that has fabulous squirrel activity every day. Daniel is in the background ready to assist. The grass is green, it's not too hot, and I've already had two cookies today. Life is good.

Love, Joey

~

About the Author

I reside in Northern California with my rescue dog and cat. I love to travel, play sports, read, and drink wine and beer. I enjoy the diversity of the world and I'm always watching people and events for story ideas. All of my stories are generated by my imagination, I don't use AI to write books.

If you would like to sign up for my bi-weekly blog and announcement of new books, please follow this link: https://www.AlecPecheBooks.com

While you're waiting for the next story, if you would be so kind as to leave a review for this book, that would be great. I appreciate all the feedback and support. Reviews buoy my spirits and stoke the fires of creativity.

If you would like to learn more about Best Friends Animal Sanctuary, please visit their website at: www.bestfriends.org/sanctuary. They have dogs, cats, birds, horses and other animals available for adoption.

Also by Alec Peche

Where Did She Go?

How Did She Get There?

<u>Dog Humor</u>

Eat, Play, Poop: Letters to my parents from camp

www.ingramcontent.com/pod-product-compliance
Lightning Source LLC
Chambersburg PA
CBHW071011120626
46546CB00003B/1032